Leaded Glass

by Paula Phillips

Capture the romance of Tiffany glass. Innovative style and simple lines provide a fresh, modern look that is always in style.

MATERIALS:
Glass piece • Stained glass paint (Crystal Clear and assorted colors) • Instant Lead Lines ⅛" • Liquid Leading • Glass paint applicator tool (or a brush)

INSTRUCTIONS:
Trace the pattern onto a piece of paper. Tape the pattern inside the glass. Apply Instant Lead Lines over lines in the drawing. Apply a dot of Liquid Leading at all intersections of the Instant Lead Lines to hold them in place and fill in any gaps. Let

1. Apply Instant Leading to the glass.

2. Apply a dot of Liquid Leading at each intersection of the leading lines.

3. Apply glass paint to each area of the design.

dry for at least one hour. • Using the spoon end of the applicator tool (or a brush), spoon paint into a section to be colored. Use the other end of the applicator tool to spread the paint into the area and to smooth out the paint. Be sure to put enough paint into the sections to fill in the lead lines. • Rinse the applicator tool between each color. • Apply the Crystal Clear Transparent paint in all areas not painted with paint colors (it will give a glass look). • Let the project dry and cure following the paint manufacturer's instructions.

Vase with Flower motif - 3" x 4" x 6" tall
Stained Glass Vase - 3" x 4" x 6"
Candle Holder - 2" diameter, 2¾" tall

Simple Sponge Art

by Paula Phillips

Now you can have unique tableware to celebrate every season and every holiday. Because these dishes are painted on the back of the plate and the outside of the glass, they are safe to use.

MATERIALS:
Glass piece • Air Dry Enamel glass paint (assorted colors) • Compressed sponges • Small round detail brush
INSTRUCTIONS:

Tape a pattern UNDER THE FRONT of the glass plate. You will be painting on the back of the plate.

Use the brush to paint dots and details. Let dry.

Use the small round brush to paint additional details such as stems, vines and outlines.

Trace small patterns onto compressed sponges and cut them out with scissors. Run sponge shapes under water so they will expand. Squeeze until almost dry.

Dip sponge into paint. Press sponge onto glass to apply the design. Dip in paint again for each design.

Rinse sponge well. Let dry.

Follow paint manufacturer's instructions for drying and curing times.

Dinner Plates - 10" round

Note - You will be painting on the WRONG SIDE OF A PLATE, so that you can eat from the front side and not touch the paint. To do this, you will need to paint in reverse order as shown above.

Details - Paint small details such as dots, buttons, eyes, mouth and seeds first.

Next paint details that are in the front such as leaves, rind, hat, and arms on the underside of the glass.

Let dry.

Note - Sponge larger designs such as strawberries, watermelons, leaves, checkerboard and snowman right over the details on the design.

Let dry.

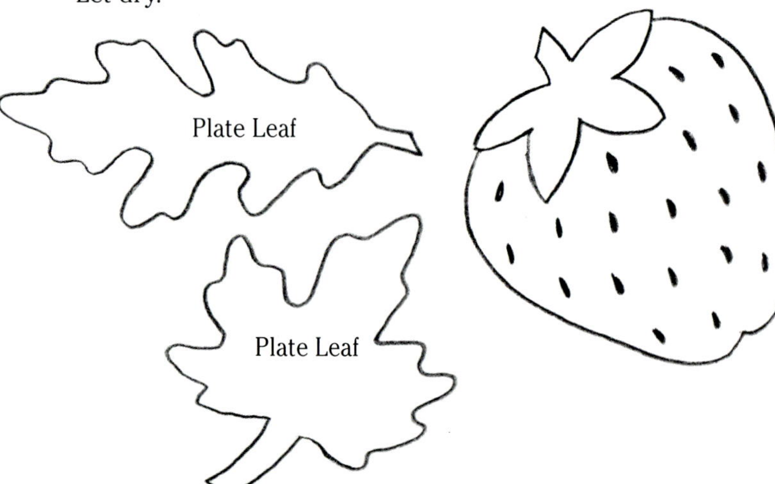

Patterns for Sponge Art

1. Draw a design on the back of Contact paper. Punch out the circles.

2. Cut out the remaining stencil design with a craft knife on a cutting mat.

3. Remove protective paper then smooth Contact paper stencil against the glass.

4. Stipple etching cream through the stencil. Let dry. Apply a second coat. Let dry.

Etching on Glass

by Paula Phillips

Create something extraordinary and beautiful by adding an elegant etched motif. You can turn inexpensive glass into exquisite designer tableware with this simple technique.

Be sure to make a few extras as gifts for family and friends.

MATERIALS:

Glass piece • Air dry glass enamel for etching • Small soft bristle flat brush • Contact paper • Glass cutting mat • Craft knife • Hole punch

INSTRUCTIONS:

Cut a stencil from Contact paper, remembering that the areas covered by the contact paper will not be etched.

Adhere Contact paper to the glass, smoothing out the bumps.

Brush glass enamel etching cream over the glass and let it dry for 1 hour. Brush on a second coat and let it dry for 10 days before removing stencil.

Use the craft knife to gently cut along the edges of the Contact paper where you brushed the enamel, and then carefully pull off the Contact paper at an angle. Use the craft knife to clean up the edges as needed.

Before washing, allow the piece to dry and cure following the manufacturer's instructions.

Etched Votive Candle Holder - 2" diameter, 2¾" tall
Etched Salt & Pepper Shakers - 1¾" x 1¾" x 4" tall
Etched Tea Glass - 2⅝" diameter, 6" tall
Etched Wine Glass - 3" diameter, 7" tall

Amber Beaded Collar

SIZE: 4" diameter, 5½" tall
INSTRUCTIONS:
Make caged beads. Tuck wire ends in bead holes.
String caged beads with smaller E-beads on stretchy cord to fit around the container. Tie cord in a knot and pull the ends back through the larger beads.

Spiral Flower Bowl

SIZE: 4" diameter, 4" tall
INSTRUCTIONS:
Wrap wire around a round dowel stick to fit the top of the bowl. Remove spiral from the stick by slipping it off the end.
Thread ribbon through the coils and tie.
Glue a flat marble to the bowl.
Shape wire spirals with beads, adhere to glass.

Tall Bottle

SIZE: 1½" x 1½" x 7½"
INSTRUCTIONS:
Shape wire figure '8's' to fit the bottle neck. Twist the wire ends together.
Make caged beads. Make small loops with wire ends at the top and bottom of the bead. Attach caged beads to the figure '8's' with lengths of wire.

Wire and Beads

by Paula Phillips
Turn ordinary glass containers into eye-catching decorations. The transparent quality of glass is the perfect backdrop for displaying the sparkle of metal and beads.

BASIC MATERIALS:
Glass piece • 24 gauge Silver wire (or thicker if possible) • Beads • Round dowel stick • Pliers (Round-nose, Needle-nose) • Wire cutters • E6000 adhesive
for Glass Bowl: Flat back marble

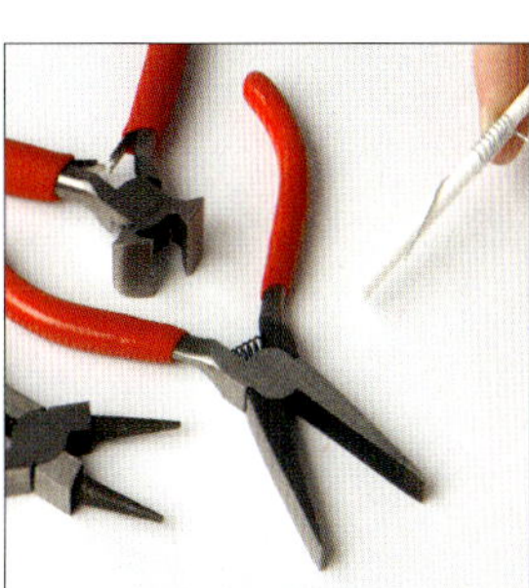

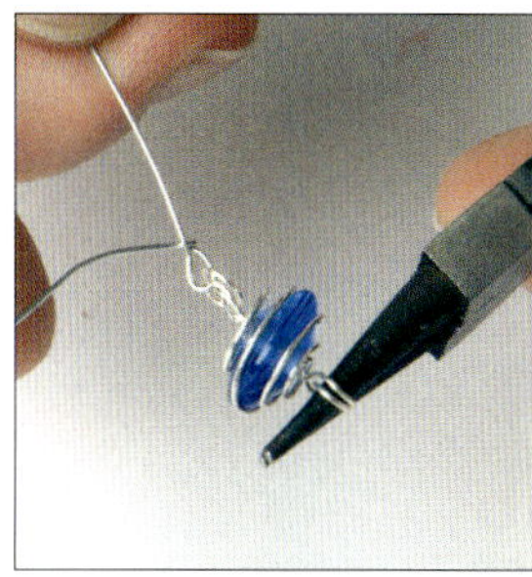

Spiral Wire: Wrap wire around a round dowel stick. Slip off the end.

Figure '8': use pliers to shape figure '8s' with a length of wire.

Caged Beads: Wrap wire around a bead to form a cage.

1. Tape a stencil in place.

2. Dab paint through the stencil.

Large Flower Zinnia Jar
SIZE: 6" diameter, 5½" tall
INSTRUCTIONS:

Tape the top and bottom of the jar with masking tape to keep the stripe straight. Paint a Pink stripe between the pieces of tape. Let dry. Peel off tape.

Tape the large stencil to the glass. Dab paint through the stencil. Let dry. Remove the stencil.

Tape a smaller stencil to glass taking care to avoid taping over previously painted areas. Dab another color of paint through the stencil. Let dry. Remove the stencil. Repeat for the center dot.

Dot around the flower centers with the handle of a brush. Paint tendrils. Let dry and cure following the paint manufacturer's instructions.

Stencil Designs

by Cyndi Hansen

Stencils open a world of possibilities for painting on glass. Available in every imaginable theme, you can match your motif to your party, breakfast room, or dressing table to create a beautiful collection of decorative bottles, containers, and tableware that your family and guests are sure to enjoy.

These items make great gifts too!

BASIC MATERIALS:
Glass piece
Stained glass paints
(assorted colors)
Stencil designs
Small sponge dabber
Paintbrushes (Fine line
and flat)
Masking tape

for Cutting a Stencil:
Clear Contact paper
Craft knife

for Words:
Rubber stamps (words)
Tsukineko StazOn ink
Clear medium
Cotton swab
Rubbing alcohol

Words Perfume Bottle

SIZE: 3" diameter, 4" tall
INSTRUCTIONS:

Stamp words on the bottle with a rubber stamp and *Tsukineko* Black StazOn ink. Keep alcohol and swabs on hand for cleaning up smears. Let dry for 30 minutes. Paint over stamped design with Clear medium to seal. Let dry.

Paint dots with Stained glass paint. Let dry.

Add small dots and swirls with a paintbrush. Let dry and cure following the paint manufacturer's instructions.

Rose Perfume Bottle

SIZE: 1¼" x 3¾" x 5" tall
INSTRUCTIONS:
To Make Your Own Stencil:
Draw a design on contact paper, cut out the design with a craft knife.

Adhere stencil to the front of bottle. Paint design with Stained glass paint. Let dry for 15 minutes and then peel off Contact paper. Paint highlights on the design. Let dry and cure following the paint manufacturer's instructions.

Carafe and Juice Glasses

CARAFE SIZE: 3½" diameter, 10¾" tall
JUICE GLASS SIZE: 3" diameter, 3½" tall
MATERIALS:
Glass Carafe and 4 juice glasses • Stained glass paints (assorted colors) • Stencil design (purchase a design or use a craft knife to cut your own from plastic stencil material) • Fine line paintbrush • Small sponge dabber
INSTRUCTIONS:

Tape a stencil outside glass.

Use a sponge dabber to dab paint through the holes in the stencil. TIP: Texture in the larger areas is good.

Dab paint for the dots.

TIP: Avoid applying paint near the rim of glass where lips would touch. Dry and cure following the paint manufacturer's instructions.

Simple Paint and Dip Dots

by Paula Phillips

It's so easy to personalize color, style, and motif when you are the designer. You can decorate jars and vases to fill with a favorite bath salt, potpourri, home-made cookies, or candy for an attractive centerpiece or thoughtful 'thinking of you' or 'thank you' gift.

MATERIALS:
Glass piece • Stain glass paints (assorted colors) • Air dry Perm Enamel glass paint • Paintbrushes (Small and Detail) • Toothpicks
INSTRUCTIONS:

Trace and cut out the pattern. Place the pattern inside the jar and tape it to the glass.

Paint the designs onto the glass using the pattern as your guide. Each design may take 2-3 coats of paint to get the desired effect. TIP - Paint in sections on the glass and allow each section to dry completely before moving to the next section to keep the paint from running. Let dry and cure following the manufacturer's instructions.

Mistakes can be repaired by applying nail polish remover with a toothpick or cotton swab, using a toothpick to remove paint when it is still wet and using a craft knife to gently scratch off paint once it is dry, but not cured.

Blue Bonnets on Small Vase - 3" diameter, 5" tall
   by Cyndi Hansen

Votive (Butterfly & Flower) - 2" diameter, 2¾" tall
Round Glass Container - 3¾" x 4⅞" tall
Votive with Dog - 2½" diameter, 3" tall
Herb Bottle with Cork - 1½" x 1½" x 7" tall
Votive with Hearts - 2½" diameter, 3" tall
Votive with Flower Garden - 2½" dia, 2½" tall
Ivy Bowl with Strawberries - 4" dia, 5½" tall

Votive (Butterfly & Flower)

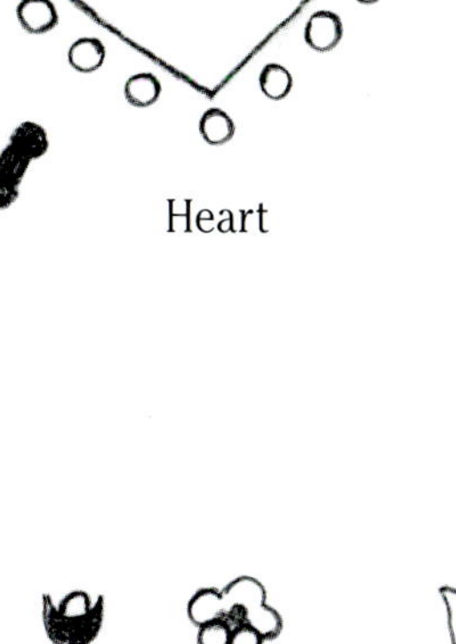

Heart

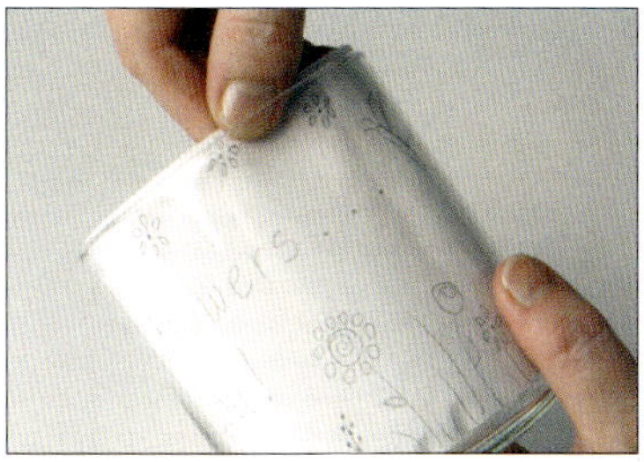

1. Tape pattern inside the container to be painted.

2. Make dots with the end of the paintbrush or a toothpick. Dip tool in paint then press dots.

3. Paint small lines and stems with a paintbrush.

Pansy

Tulip

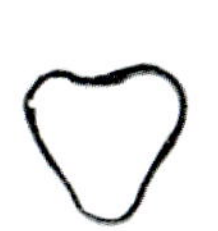

Strawberry Votive

Lily of the Valley

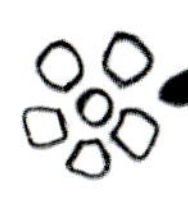

Daisy

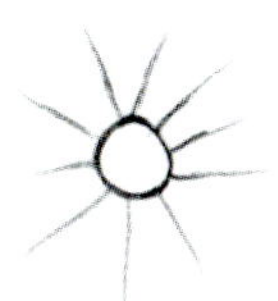

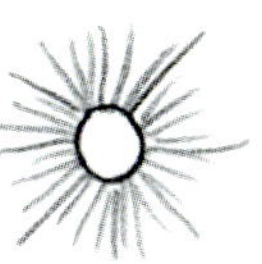

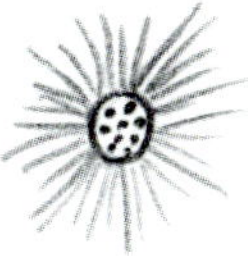

Sunflower

Dog

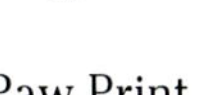

Paw Print

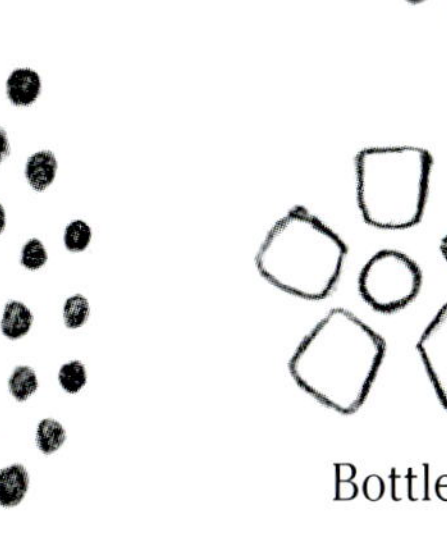

Bottle

Doodles and Swirls

by Cyndi Hansen
Doodles and swirls are timeless designs that can be found even in ancient ruins.
*   These appealing designs are drawn with metallic and Black pens for a gorgeous effect.*

Copper Cylinder Candle Holder
SIZE: 3½" diameter, 6" tall
MATERIALS:
Glass piece • Copper leafing pen • Copper metallic glass paint • Copper metal foil adhesive tape

Painting

Whether you prefer dramatic color or that home-made cozy feeling, painting on glass allows you to express your personality.

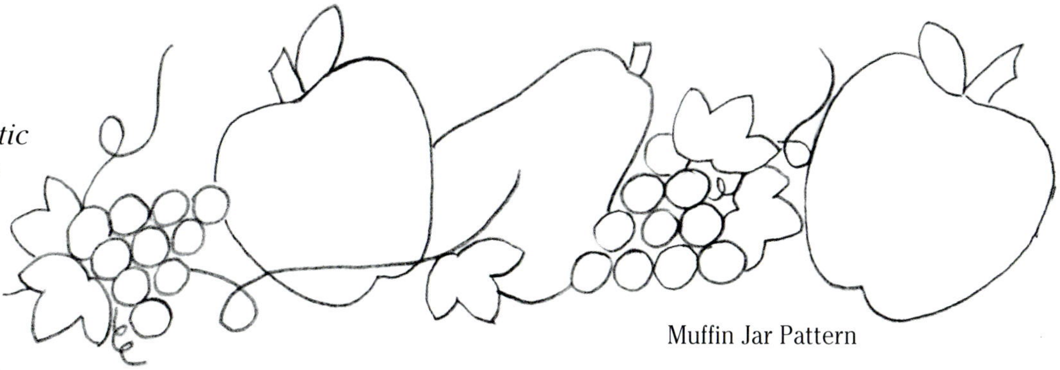

Muffin Jar Pattern

Basic Instructions

Tape the pattern inside the glass.

Paint glass in sections. Allow each section to dry completely before moving to the next section.

For the larger designs, use the spoon end of the tool or a brush to apply paint into the middle of the design, then smooth paint out to the shape of the pattern. After the design is filled in with paint, comb back and forth with the tool to evenly disperse the paint in the design.

1. Place a pattern inside a jar.

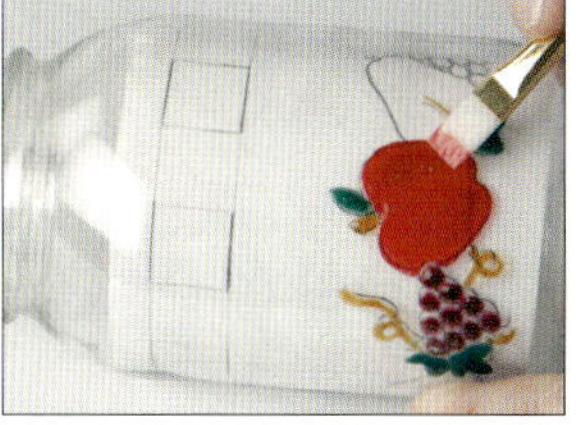

2. Paint colors on the jar with a small brush.

3. Assemble materials and screw the lid in place.

Muffin Jar

by Paula Phillips

SIZE: 3¼" diameter, 7" tall

MATERIALS:
Canning jar with lid
Stained glass paints
  (assorted colors)
Glass paint applicator
  tool (or brush)
6" square Red print
  fabric and small
  piece of batting
Paper tag, twine, pin
Muffin mix
Pink tacky tape

INSTRUCTIONS:
Paint the design on glass and allow to dry and cure.

Apply pink tape to the edge of the lid. Cover lid with batting and fabric. Place lid into the jar ring.

Fill jar with muffin mix. Write a recipe on a tag and tie to the top with a pin.

Hand Painted Square Vase

by Cyndi Hansen

SIZE: 2¾" x 8" x 8"

MATERIALS:
Square glass vase
Stained glass paints
  (assorted opaque
  colors)
Fine line paintbrush
Paintbrush handle
  as a dotter

Dragonfly
Flower
Leaf & Swirl pattern for page 17
Diamonds pattern for page 17

Framed Window Hangings
- 5½" x 7½"

MATERIALS:
Black frame with a 4" x 6" glass
Stained glass paint colors
Liquid Leading
Glass paint applicator tool (or brush)
Masking tape

INSTRUCTIONS:
Take the glass out of the frame, clean it, and tape a pattern to the back side of the glass.

Apply Liquid Leading over the lines of the pattern on the top of glass. Let dry for 24 hours.

Paint areas of the design. If the applicator tool is not small enough to push the paint into the small areas, use a toothpick.

Let dry following the paint manufacturer's instructions.

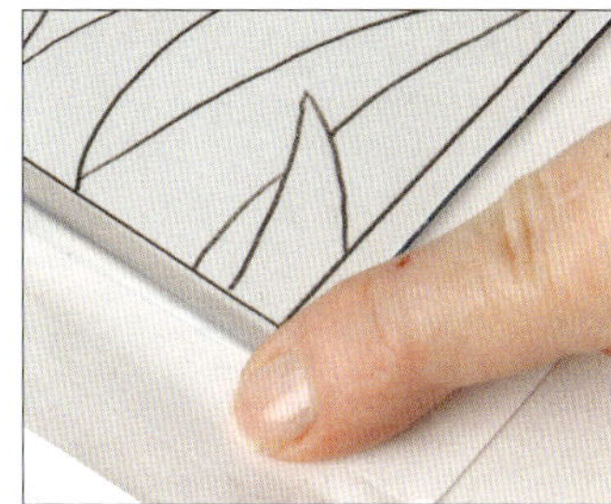

1. Trace or draw a pattern. Tape the pattern under a piece of glass.

2. Apply Liquid Lead on top of the glass. Clean up any smudges with a craft knife.

3. Paint a color in each shape. Let dry. Place glass in a frame.

Stained Glass Windows

by Paula Phillips
Fill your favorite space with color and light. The wonderful thing about stained glass is that it looks equally stunning from both sides. You will really enjoy this simple yet beautiful project.

Metal Leafing

by Cyndi Hansen
Draw attention to your photograph by surrounding it with glittering leafing. Create intricate patterns with a leafing pen and add a silver background with sheet leafing for a uniquely beautiful finish.

Silver Leaf Shadowbox Frame - 10" x 10" x 1¾" deep
MATERIALS:
Shadowbox frame with glass • Decorative papers • Photo • Liquid Gold paint pen • Silver leaf sheets • Metal leaf adhesive • Sandpaper • Paintbrushes (Flat, Soft) • Pattern • Adhesive foam dots
INSTRUCTIONS:
Lay pattern under glass. Use a Gold pen to draw over design. Let dry for 1 hour.

On the wrong side of the glass, use a flat brush to paint leaf adhesive around edges of glass and over the design area. Lay Silver leaf over adhesive. Remove excess with a soft brush. Sand if desired.

Adhere papers and photo to back of frame, reassemble the box.

1. Place glass over a pattern. Paint Gold on the front of the glass.

2. Apply adhesive over an area on the back of the glass.

3. Carefully place a sheet of Silver leaf over adhesive. Use a soft brush to tap it in place.

4. Rough up the surface slightly with a fine sanding paper or block.

Metal Leafing on Glass

Add a touch of old world elegance with sparkling Silver leafing. Silver and Black combine in a bold and graphic design that will complement any modern home while the warm and inviting copper swirls soften the environment for a romantic candlelit evening.

Copper Leaf
Ivy Bowl with Candle

- 4" diameter, 5½" tall

MATERIALS:
Glass ivy bowl • Liquid Gold paint pen • Copper leaf sheets • Metal leaf adhesive • Stained glass paint(Orange) • Sea sponge • Clear medium • Paintbrushes (Flat, Soft)

INSTRUCTIONS:

Use a damp sea sponge to apply paint all over the outside of bowl. Let dry for 1 hour.

Tape leaf patterns (page 14) inside the bowl. Paint leaf adhesive over the leaves on the front of bowl.

Lay Copper leaf on glass over glue and use a soft brush to smooth and remove excess.

Let dry for several hours. Apply Clear medium over leafing to seal.

Use a Liquid Gold pen to draw swirls on glass and to paint the top edge of jar. Let dry for several hours. Apply Clear medium over entire jar to seal.

Silver & Black
Topiary Jar

- 5" diameter, 9" tall

MATERIALS:
Glass jar • Silver leaf sheets • Metal leaf adhesive • Silver tape • air dry Glass paint (Black) • Clear medium • Paintbrushes (Flat, Soft) • Glue pen

INSTRUCTIONS:

Tape diamonds pattern (page 14) inside the glass jar and underneath the base. Paint diamonds with Black paint. Let dry.

Use a flat brush and Leaf adhesive to paint inside the rim of jar behind the diamonds.

Lay Silver leaf on glass over adhesive and use a soft brush to smooth and remove excess.

Let dry for several hours. Apply Clear medium over leafing to seal.

Apply Silver tape down center sides and around the center of jar. Apply Silver tape around rims and around the top.

Mosaic on Glass

by Paula Phillips

Mosaic tiles add irresistible texture, gorgeous color, pearlescent luster and interesting patterns to ordinary glass. Make something fabulous today!

MATERIALS:
Glass piece • Glass flat back marbles or flat mosaic tiles • E6000 adhesive
OPTIONAL: Mosaic grout
INSTRUCTIONS:

Adhere marbles or tiles to the glass with E6000 adhesive. You will need to adhere one side at a time then let the adhesive dry for at least two hours. Adhere marbles or tiles to another side. Repeat. Let dry.

Optional: Mix grout and water following the manufacturer's instructions. Press grout into the spaces between the marbles or tiles. Let dry for 10 - 15 minutes. Wipe with a damp sponge in a circular motion. Wait 5 - 10 minutes and wipe again. Repeat until all grout is removed from the marbles or tiles and the grout is smooth.

Blue Vase - 3" x 3⅞" x 5⅞" tall
Blue Marbles - 3⅝" diameter, 3" tall
Square Vase - 2½" x 2½" x 8" tall
Green Tiles - 3" diameter, 4" tall

Blue Vase -
MATERIALS:
Glass vase • Glass flat back marbles • Stained glass paint (Light Blue and White Pearl) • Glass paint applicator tool (or brush) • Adhesive-back lead line ⅛" wide • E6000 adhesive
INSTRUCTIONS:

Mix together equal parts of the Light Blue and White Pearl glass paint.

Spoon or apply the paint onto one side of the vase. Only paint one side at a time. Use the pointed end of the tool to draw a swirl pattern through the paint.

Let dry for at least 24 hours.

Repeat for the remaining sides of the vase.

Adhere a lead line for the flower stem.

Adhere flat marbles in a flower pattern.

1. Attach glass tiles or marbles with E6000 or Goop glue.

2. Let each side of the glass set for an hour or more until the glue holds.